There are lots of different types of owls, around 200 different species! Owls live in every continent except Antarctica. They are nocturnal animals, which means they are active at night. They have big eyes and flat, round faces.

Owls can hear very well. This helps them search for prey that is invisible under leaves or snow on the ground. The sound doesn't have to be loud, the owl will hear any soft, tiny sound!

Owls hunt insects, earthworms, birds and small mammals, such as a mouse or a vole. They jump down from a tree branch and pounce on their prey. They catch it with their strong talons.

The brown owl is found in woodlands. It nests in a tree hole so it can protect its eggs and young from predators.

The snowy owl lives in the Arctic. The males are white, and the females have white faces but their bodies are speckled with brown and black. This helps them blend into the snowy background.

Snowy owls eat lemmings, which are small rodents. In fact, they eat vast amounts of lemmings, up to five a day! They also hunt rabbits, birds and fish.

The powerful owl is found in Australia. It is a very big owl, with a long tail and a small head. When it hoots, it makes a "whoo-hoo" sound.

A quirky thing about owls is that they can turn their heads almost all the way round.